Move & Learn
MATH ACTIVITIES

by Heljä Robinson, Robert Wolffe,
and Jean Marie Grant

SCHOLASTIC
PROFESSIONAL BOOKS

New York • Toronto • London • Auckland • Sydney
Mexico City • New Delhi • Hong Kong • Buenos Aires

Dedication

To you, the teacher, as you work in your classroom to bring alive the joys of learning math in creative and constructive ways.

Cover design by Susan Kass

Cover artwork by Viki Woodworth

Interior design by Sydney Wright

Interior artwork by Cary Pillo

Interior photographs by Heljä Robinson, Robert Wolffe, and Jean Marie Grant

ISBN: 0-439-30358-3

1 2 3 4 5 6 7 8 9 10   40   09 08 07 06 05 04 03 02

Contents

Introduction 5
Supporting Math Learners 7
Linking Learning to the NCTM Standards 8

Activities

Number and Operations

Moving to the Beat 9
using one-to-one correspondence

Beanbag-Toss Addition 10
identifying number families, fluency

Giant-Stretch Subtraction 12
subtracting, relating operations

Shaping Subtraction 14
fluency, relating operations

Parachute Pop-Offs 16
subtracting, relating operations

Play-Act Math Facts 18
subtracting, relating operations

Musical Fraction Sheets 20
identifying fractions

Patterning and Early Algebra

Numbo 22
following patterns

Create-a-Dance 23
constructing, following patterns

Anatomy Patterns 24
reconstructing patterns

Pitter-Patter Poems 26
identifying pattern connections

Skip Relay 28
skip-counting patterns

Playing Out Problems 30
identifying variables

Geometry

Ribbon Dance 32
identifying spatial terms

Bend-a-Bit Shape Making 34
visualizing

Diamond Dance 36
developing spatial sense

Mystery Shapes 38
sorting, classifying

Sliding Along 40
identifying shapes

We Can Be... 42
identifying properties

Trans-Dance 44
identifying orientation

Measurement

Ring Around 47
using non-standardized units

Cocoon 48
estimating

Galloping Giants 50
using non-standardized units

I Am Fastest When... 52
predicting

Treasure Measure 54
estimating

Data Analysis and Probability

Hungry Birds 56
sorting, classifying

Venn Catcher 58
problem solving, comparing

Swirly Streamers 60
exploring probability

Musical Graph 62
reading simple line graphs

Wiggle Bars 64
sorting, using bar graphs

> *"Students must learn mathematics with understanding, actively building new knowledge from experience and prior knowledge."*
>
> —*National Council of Teachers of Mathematics, 2000*

ntroduction

The teacher-tested, interactive activities in *Move & Learn Math Activities* invite young students of all learning styles to have fun exploring addition, subtraction, patterns, shapes, measuring, and more—as well as help them meet the National Council of Teachers of Mathematics (NCTM) standards.

Move & Learn Math Activities has been written to help you, the classroom teacher, tune into and build upon children's natural channels of active learning by providing effective, concrete ways to teach math through movement—with activities such as Beanbag-Toss Addition, Giant-Stretch Subtraction, and Treasure Measure.

The thirty activities in this book reflect current research in education and have been especially designed to complement your early childhood curriculum. They provide math-learning experiences that help children make important experiential connections among different areas of their cognitive, physical, and socio-emotional development. Beyond that, movement is a powerful tool to help children learn math. It's a way to guide students through the process of becoming "educated, confident, powerful, spirited human beings" (Hackney, 1998, 26). The activities in this book support learning by:

◆ complementing all learning styles.

◆ enhancing understanding of key math concepts.

◆ integrating learning with music and imagination.

◆ strengthening emotional intelligence (Goleman, 1996), boosting self-esteem, self-awareness, and social skills.

◆ accessing physical need for activity in constructive, meaningful ways.

◆ helping to develop balance, posture, respiration, muscle strength, stamina, agility, relaxation skills, and attention span.

◆ inviting creativity and meeting the needs of belonging, freedom, power, and enjoyment (Glasser, 1990).

◆ supporting a joyful learning setting through the release of endorphins, the "feel-good" chemicals in the brain (Howard, 1994).

◆ providing creative opportunities for children to explore movement-related aptitudes, including:

  ＊ locomotor movements—running, galloping, skipping
  ＊ non-locomotor movements—starting, stopping, swinging
  ＊ manipulative movements—throwing, tossing
  ＊ perceptual skills—eye-hand and eye-foot coordination, visual and tactile senses
  ＊ physical fitness—flexibility, strength
  ＊ combined movements—creative games, activities with equipment (Carnes, 1983).

Making Connections for the Learner

Learning with the body is a way of reinforcing both the meaning (semantic) and procedural memory pathways, helping learners recall content that might not have initial appeal to them. Movement is a motivator.

Movement activities aren't just fun, they're a great way for students to learn math!

> "Real learning—the kind of learning that establishes meaningful connections for the learner—is not complete until there is some output, some physical expression, personal expression of thought. Much of learning involves the establishment of skills that enable us to express our knowledge. . . . As we build these skills we use the muscles of our bodies, establishing neuromuscular routes as well as their ties to cognitive routes. Learning is not all in your head. The active muscular expression of learning is an important ingredient of that learning." (Hannaford, 1995, 87)

About the Authors

The authors of *Move & Learn Math Activities* are associate professors of education at Bradley University in Peoria, Illinois. With a wealth of experience teaching both children and teachers, the authors share their innovative ideas through writing and in-service workshops around the country.

Heljä Robinson, Ph.D., has been an early childhood teacher in both the United States and Finland. She has worked extensively to help teachers reflect on classroom practices, and is a current William T. Kemper Teaching Excellence Fellow. She is the author of *The Ethnography of Empowerment: The Transformative Power of Classroom Interaction* (Taylor & Francis, 1994).

Robert Wolffe, Ed.D., has 14 years experience teaching children in second through fifth grades. In addition, he has worked with pre-service teachers to deepen their understanding of fundamental math and science concepts through effective pedagogy. He recently completed an appointment as the William T. Kemper Teaching Excellence Fellow.

Jean Marie Grant, Ph.D., has taught math at a variety of grade levels in Greece, Germany, Malaysia, and the United States. Her present work with pre-service and in-service math teachers addresses the math processes as stated by the National Council of Teachers of Mathematics.

upporting Math Learners

In supporting the overall development of children, the math activities in this book support academic success. (See page 8 for a complete skills matrix.) Each activity in this collection comes complete with a summary of skills and concepts covered, step-by-step directions, grouping tips, material lists, and photos that guide you every step of the way. To help make lesson planning easier, you'll find each activity has been organized into the following format:

◆ STEPPING UP: The Math Behind the Movement—Describes the activity's math objective and includes a short overview of the learning embedded in the activity.

◆ JUMPING IN: The Activity—Provides step-by-step instructions and photos.

◆ MOVING RIGHT ALONG: Assessment—Offers key questions to ask your students and suggestions for checking their understanding.

◆ TAKING IT FURTHER: Extensions—Recommends ways to offer children new learning challenges and propel student learning even further.

Professional Resources

Carnes, Cliff. 1983. *Awesome Elementary Physical Education Activities*. Carmichael, CA: Cliff Carnes.

Glasser, William. 1990. *The Quality School*. New York, NY: Harper & Row.

Goleman, Daniel P. 1995. *Emotional Intelligence: Why It Can Matter More Than IQ*. New York, NY: Bantam Books.

Goleman, Daniel P. 1998. *Working With Emotional Intelligence*. New York, NY: Bantam Books.

Hackney, P. 1998. Moving Wisdom. *In Context*. 18, Winter 1988: 26–27.

Hannaford, Carla. 1995. *Smart Moves: Why Learning Is Not All in Your Head*. New York, NY: Great Ocean Publishers.

Howard, Pierce J. 1994. *The Owner's Manual for the Brain: Everyday Applications from Mind-Brain Research*. Austin, TX: Leornian Press.

National Council of Teachers of Mathematics. To order the Principles and Standards for School Mathematics, call 800/235-7566, e-mail orders@nctm.org, or go online to http://www.nctm.org.

Robinson, H. & Wolffe, R. 1996. Brain-Friendly Classrooms: Teaching for the Whole Child. *Illinois School Research and Development Journal*. 331: 3–6.

TIP!
Sucessful Transitions

Help young children make successful transitions to movement activities. Start with brief math-movement experiences in order to establish classroom management routines that work for your students. Consider:

✱ Setting aside a special time of the day for math-movement activities. That way students know what to expect and when to expect it.

✱ Playing a few notes on an instrument. Tell students: "When you hear this music, you'll know it's time for our math-movement activity to begin."

✱ Asking students to show they're ready to participate by putting themselves in a "ready position," such as: standing with their hands on their hips, sitting on the circle-time rug, and so on.

✱ Inviting reluctant participants to be DJs, pushing the *play* button on the CD player when it's time for the class to begin the activity. Students will enjoy helping the class prepare for the activity and you'll appreciate the way music refocuses the class's attention in a positive way.

Linking Learning to the NCTM Standards

This book is organized around and supports the NCTM Content Standards: Number and Operations, Patterning and Early Algebra, Geometry, Measurement, and Data Analysis and Probability. Each activity invites students to explore problem solving and reasoning in a natural, playful manner that allows for problem definition, multiple solutions, and reflection on questions such as, "How do you know it is true?" To see how the activities in this book have been correlated with the NCTM standards, refer to the skills matrix below.

Connections to the NCTM Standards

Activity Titles	Number and Operations	Patterns, Functions, and Algebra	Geometry and Spatial Sense	Measurement	Data Analysis, Statistics, & Probability	Problem Solving	Reasoning and Proof	Communication	Connections	Representation
Moving to the Beat	•							•		•
Beanbag-Toss Addition	•							•		•
Giant-Step Subtraction	•							•		•
Shaping Subtraction	•				•			•		•
Parachute Pop-Offs	•					•				
Play-Act Math Facts	•					•		•		•
Musical Fraction Sheets	•					•		•		•
Numbo		•	•							•
Create-a-Dance		•						•		•
Anatomy Patterns		•				•		•	•	•
Pitter-Patter Poems		•				•		•		•
Skip Relay		•						•	•	•
Playing Out Problems		•				•	•	•		
Ribbon Dance			•					•		•
Bend-a-Bit Shape Making			•			•		•		•
Diamond Dance			•					•	•	•
Mystery Shapes			•				•	•		•
Sliding Along			•			•	•	•		
We Can Be . . .			•			•	•	•		•
Trans-Dance			•					•		•
Ring Around				•		•	•			•
Cocoon				•				•		•
Galloping Giants	•			•		•		•		•
I Am Fastest When . . .				•		•		•		
Treasure Measure				•		•	•			
Hungry Birds		•			•			•		
Venn Catcher		•			•					•
Swirly Streamers					•	•			•	
Musical Graph					•	•		•		•
Wiggle Bars					•	•	•	•		•

oving to the Beat

STEPPING UP: **The Math Behind the Movement**

By identifying the sounds of rhythm instruments and creating interpretive movements, children practice counting and listening skills. Matching body movements to their auditory experience, students translate one representational model into another (one-to-one correspondence).

JUMPING IN: **The Activity**

Choose instruments that have distinct sounds. Ask students to listen as you play a simple rhythm. Tell them to describe sounds they hear. Then play the rhythm again. Have children use their bodies to show the number of beats they hear.

Select a different instrument and play a different rhythm. Or choose one child at a time to play an instrument to a beat while the rest of the class listens. As a class:

1. Clap the rhythm.

2. Think of other ways of showing the rhythm through movement.

3. Take turns in different roles—the musician who creates the beat and the movers expressing what they hear.

4. Discuss which is easier, recognizing or creating the beat.

As a class, brainstorm ways to check that the movers are moving as often as the beat suggests.

MOVING RIGHT ALONG: **Assessment**

Have students create written records of their experience by drawing pictures to the beat instead of moving to the beat. For example, a crisscross could mean *clap*. Help them check for accuracy by asking: *Can we move according to what we see in the picture? What clues about moving do these pictures give us?*

TAKING IT FURTHER: **Extensions**

✪ Ask children to count and move at the same time. Try this at transition times, moving from place to place around the school building. Or try it outdoors, changing the tempo often.

Math Skills and Concepts
one-to-one correspondence
counting
communication
representation

Grouping
whole group
small groups

Movement
locomotor—clapping, jumping
hopping, etc.

Materials
◆ rhythm instruments—drum, rhythm sticks, xylophone, etc.

Beanbag-Toss Addition

STEPPING UP: The Math Behind the Movement

Develop students' number fluency and enjoy the time-honored fun of tossing beanbags! Before you begin, have students identify all possible addition combinations that make up a particular number family. For example, for the 5 family, students would toss a total of five beanbags at the target shape. Where the beanbags land in relation to the target shape determines the number-family addition sentence: 0 "in" + 5 "out," 1 "in" + 4 "out," 2 "in" + 3 "out," 3 "in" + 2 "out," 4 "in" + 1 "out," and 5 "in" + 0 "out."

JUMPING IN: The Activity

Model what your students are to do in this activity. Begin by creating a target on the floor with masking tape or yarn. The target should be a closed shape, about a foot in diameter. (Have younger students form simple shapes such as squares, circles, or triangles.) Show students how to toss the beanbags one at a time at the target shape. Some beanbags will land inside the shape and some outside. Have students record each combination in an addition sentence format. For example, 1 "in" + 4 "out" = 5.

Divide your class into small groups of three students each. Provide each group with the number of beanbags for the number family that the class is working on. Then ask each group to:

1. Create a target shape on the floor using masking tape or yarn.

2. Select one group member to toss each beanbag at a target shape.

3. Select a second group member to count the number of beanbags that land inside the target shape and the number of beanbags that land outside the target shape.

4. Select a third group member to record the number sentence—the number "in" plus the number "out" equals the number of beanbags in all (the specified number family).

Math Skills and Concepts
number fluency
communication
representation

Grouping
small groups of three

Movement
using manipulatives
perceptual skills

Materials
◆ beanbags
◆ masking tape or yarn
◆ recording materials (paper and pencils)

5. Have students alternate jobs and identify the other number sentences for the number family.

MOVING RIGHT ALONG:
Assessment

Observe students as they count and record their beanbag-toss totals. Listen as they describe which results are repeated and which addition combinations haven't been recorded. Then review each group's written record of number combinations. Confirm that students have identified all possible number sentences for the number family you've selected.

TAKING IT FURTHER: Extensions

⊛ Ask students to rewrite the addition sentences as subtraction sentences. For example: 5 "total" – 1 "out" = 4 "in," and 5 "total" – 3 "out" = 2 "in," and so on.

⊛ Give students practice developing their graphing skills. Ask them to record the number of times each number sentence (0 "in" + 5 "out" = 5 "total") occurred during their beanbag tossing. Have each group bar-graph the results.

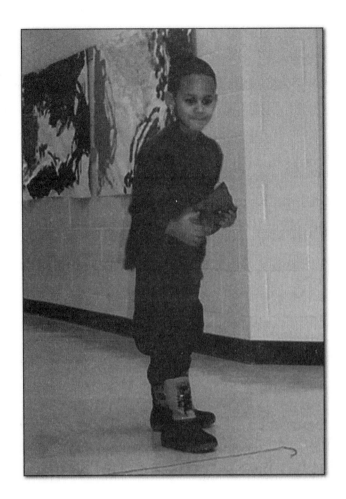

Giant-Stretch Subtraction

STEPPING UP: The Math Behind the Movement

In addition to helping develop fluency with numbers and basic operations, Giant-Stretch Subtraction is a fun way to help children develop a sense of counting for a purpose. It invites students to begin using a number line and to explore the idea of subtraction as a missing addend. What's more, as your students work the problems mentally and then work them again on the number line, they will begin to see the relationship of subtraction as the inverse of addition.

JUMPING IN: The Activity

Before you begin, create number lines. Cut a roll of adding machine paper into several 11-foot lengths, one for each group. Draw a number line on each strip, writing the numerals 0–10 at 1-foot intervals. Then provide each group with a number line and a deck of cards for the number family on which the class is working, several index cards with numbers printed on them, a few blank index cards, and symbol cards with which to express addition sentences ("+" and "="). Have children explore the concept of addition by finding a missing addend. Encourage students to take turns within their groups as they take on the different roles of Steppers and Writers.

1. Tell the class which number family they will be using as the target number—an end point to reach on the number line.

2. The first Stepper from each group stands on the target number, waiting to hear what the first addend will be.

3. The Writer draws a number card (addend) from the deck. The Writer's job is to use that number card in an addition sentence, laying the problem out on the floor where the rest of the group can readily see the number card, the + symbol, a blank index card, an = sign card, and the answer card (the target number). For example, if your students are working on the 6 family and the Writer draws a 2, the arrangement would be like this:

$$2 \ + \ \boxed{} \ = \ 6$$

Math Skills and Concepts
fluency with subtraction
counting
communication
representation

Grouping
whole class
groups of three to four

Movement
locomotor—stepping, stretching, balancing
combined movement

Materials
◆ adding machine paper
◆ decks of numbered index cards
◆ blank index cards
◆ + and – symbol cards for each group

4. A second Stepper, setting one foot on the 0, places his or her other foot on the number drawn.

5. The first Stepper, keeping one foot on the target number, stretches the other foot to the second Stepper's foot location, the first addend. Working with the 2 + __ = 6 example from the previous page, the first Stepper has his or her feet spread from the target number (6) to the first addend (2). The second Stepper has one foot on the zero and his or her other foot on the first addend (2). The missing addend is still in question.

6. To find the missing addend, the first Stepper needs to count the spaces on the number line between his or her feet. In this case, he or she would have four spaces. The missing addend is 4.

7. The Writer finds the card from the number deck that completes the number sentence (4) and places it in his group's number sentence. The problem is complete.

8. The students in each group then alternate roles until they have created all the number sentences or addend combinations in the number family.

MOVING RIGHT ALONG: Assessment

By asking your students to explain their process and listening to them work, you'll have a window into their understanding of subtraction as solving for a missing addend. As the activity concludes, check for accuracy and completeness by scanning the number sentences each group's Writers have laid out on the floor.

TAKING IT FURTHER: Extensions

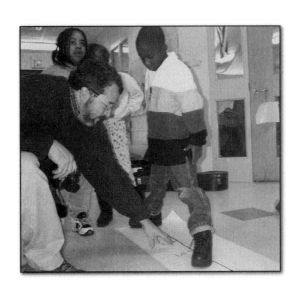

✺ Instead of subtracting, try adding! Working in pairs, have one student draw a number and take a giant step. Then have a second student draw a number and take a giant step. Finally, encourage the partners to work together to solve the addition problem. Since they will be working each problem separately (2 + 7 = 9, 4 + 1 = 5, and 3 + 3 = 6) rather than developing a whole number family (2 + 1 = 3, 2 + 2 = 4, 2 + 3 = 5, and so on), your students will be gaining valuable experience with addition. When your students are ready, invite them to work with three addends, challenging your young learners to both add and subtract.

Shaping Subtraction

STEPPING UP: The Math Behind the Movement

In Shaping Subtraction, as the children learn about the inter-relationship between addition and subtraction, they develop number fluency. Acting out the math problems they encounter lets students explore both the "taking away from" and "missing addend" approaches to subtraction. Then, as they record math sentences, word problems become subtraction stories retold with shapes and symbols. In addition, this activity helps young learners gain valuable experience solving math problems that have more than one possible solution.

JUMPING IN: The Activity

On the floor, make two large shapes from different-colored tape or yarn, such as a red triangle, a green square, a blue rectangle, or a yellow circle. Explain to students that the class will be using what they know about math families to solve math word problems. Remind them that number families are the number combinations that add up to a number. For example: 2 + 3 = 5, 1 + 4 = 5, 5 + 0 = 5.

1. Begin the activity with a story like this one: *Eight children crawled into the red triangle. How many children hopped out*

Math Skills and Concepts
number fluency
number families
problem solving
communication

Grouping
whole class
two groups

Movement
locomotor—crawling, creeping, hopping, etc.

Materials
◆ masking tape or yarn

These students are solving math word problems, making the most of their carpet's grid-like pattern.

of the triangle and into the green square, if there are five children left in the triangle?

Ask students to retell the story using their own words. Then ask: *How else could we arrange eight children in the two shapes? What math story or sentence might explain each of these arrangements?*

2. For younger children, simplify the activity by working with addition rather than subtraction. Ask students to tell the math sentence that explains what happened in the story. Have a volunteer record the math sentence on the chalkboard in symbolic or pictorial form. Or offer students math manipulatives to retell what happened in the story. Tell a story like this one: *Six children skip into the green square. If we have eight children in all, how many other children can skip into the red triangle?*

3. After discussing the math word problems and acting them out, divide the class into two groups. Have the groups take turns creating a story, moving themselves into the shapes, and recording the math sentence.

MOVING RIGHT ALONG: Assessment

Observe students as they communicate answers to the questions, make up their own stories, and record results in symbolic or pictorial form. Check for accuracy.

TAKING IT FURTHER: Extensions

✸ Have students work in groups to do a subtraction problem rather than solve for a specific number family. Invite them to practice at their own desks with manipulatives.

✸ Challenge small groups of children to work with three different shapes and addition only. Have them try using three different shapes and addition as well as subtraction.

Parachute Pop-Offs

STEPPING UP: The Math Behind the Movement

What's more fun than tossing beanbags in the air with a parachute? Catching them! Kids gain lots of practice with different mental strategies that can be used in subtraction as they calculate the number of beanbags that land on the floor after each parachute "pop." This is a great activity for supporting the take-away concept of subtraction.

JUMPING IN: The Activity

Before you begin, determine whether you want your students to practice subtraction with a particular number family or a random number. If you plan to work with a number family, set that number of beanbags aside for the parachute activity and tell students which number family you'll be working with. If you plan to select the number of beanbags randomly, invite students to add beanbags or remove them before you begin each toss.

1. Ask students to stand in a circle around the perimeter of the parachute and grasp its edges firmly with both hands.

2. Place the beanbags in the middle of the parachute. (If you are randomly selecting the number of beanbags, you may want to choose a student to count the number of beanbags aloud before each parachute toss.)

3. On the count of three, say "pop!" together. Then, lift up the parachute quickly, tossing the beanbags into the air. Use the surface of the parachute to catch as many falling beanbags as possible.

4. Collect the beanbags that fall on the floor without showing them to the children, then ask them how many are missing. Solve the subtraction problem. Discuss the strategies they used to find their answer.

Math Skills and Concepts
subtraction
reasoning

Grouping
whole class

Movement
using manipulatives

Materials
◆ parachute (or sheet)
◆ 10 beanbags (or enough beanbags for the number family you are working with)

For example: Did students add the number of beanbags remaining in the parachute until reaching the starting value? Or did they take away the number of beanbags remaining in the parachute from the number of beanbags they had at the start?

5. Invite students to discuss ways they could check whether their answers are correct. Try a few of their suggestions. Then have students verify the answer by helping you count the beanbags aloud while you position them back in the center of the parachute.

6. Repeat the tossing, calculating, and checking process several times.

MOVING RIGHT ALONG: Assessment

While students determine how many beanbags have fallen to the floor, listen to their problem-solving discussion. Consider the accuracy of their answers. Then ask students to explain their methods for solving the subtraction problem and checking their work.

Or invite students to explain how they solved the subtraction problem using paper circles to represent the parachute (or rectangles if a sheet was used) and beans to represent the beanbags. Ask students to model what happened to the beanbags after the parachute was "popped." Ask them to tell or write the number sentence that represents the subtraction problem. Observe their work and check written answers for accuracy.

TAKING IT FURTHER: Extensions

The Parachute Pop-Offs activity described above invites students to explore the take-away concept of subtraction, whereas the following extension activity challenges students to explore the comparison concept of subtraction.

✿ Place a row of beanbags on the floor equal to the original number placed on the parachute. Then line up the ones remaining on the parachute next to the original group of beanbags. Ask students to compare the number of beanbags in each set (row). Guide them to notice that the difference between the rows is equal in number to the set of beanbags that fell on the floor.

Play-Act Math Facts

STEPPING UP: The Math Behind the Movement

Play-Act Math Facts helps children tackle basic math facts through an empowering problem-solving strategy, role play. By acting out the story problems, students see answers to addition and subtraction problems as part of a real experience. They learn in a hands-on way, rather than through memorization. It's an activity that reinforces two important math concepts—that addition is the joining of sets and that subtraction can be either taking away or comparing values to find differences.

JUMPING IN: The Activity

Before you begin, check that there is enough room for children to move as they act out the stories. Share the story problem in whatever way suits your class's instructional needs, with you as the narrator or storyteller.

1. Choose your role. If you decide to play the role of the narrator, ask the class to be active listeners. As the events in the story are told, discuss with children what roles are needed. Have them play the parts of the numbers, showing what happened in the story.

Note: If you decide to be the storyteller, record important details on the board as you relate the whole story. It is especially important to record the values (3 grasshoppers + 5 grasshoppers, for example) for the children, so they can refer to them as they act out the story in small groups when the story is over. When you divide your class into groups, think about the size of the values in the problems. Each group's number depends on those values.

2. Share the story problem. Here are a few sample story problems to get you started:

• Darrel collects grasshoppers. Yesterday he found 3 and today he found 5 more. How many did he find over the last 2 days? (Watch what students do with the extraneous value of 2 as they become grasshoppers.)

• Goufan made 8 egg rolls. She put special sauce on only 3

Math Skills and Concepts
addition
subtraction
problem solving
reasoning
representation

Grouping
whole class
small groups

Movement
locomotor—skipping, running, crawling, etc.
non-locomotor—stretching, swaying, etc.

Materials
◆ recording materials (paper and pencils)
◆ manipulatives (optional)

and ate only those. How many did not have special sauce and were not eaten? (Observe take-away subtraction.)

- Saul and Megan collected cereal-box tops for their class. Megan brought 8 to school and Saul brought 5. How many more box tops did Megan bring than Saul? (This is a comparison subtraction problem that gives children practice with both inequalities and subtraction. It asks a "who brought the most" question followed by a "how many more" question.)

3. After they have heard the whole story problem, have students work in small groups to determine how to dramatize what happened and how they can become the values and show the addition or subtraction problem. Then have students act out the story and find a solution. Give children who can read a large-print copy of the story problems. They can work through the process more independently while you circulate among groups, guiding students in their efforts.

4. Repeat the process with other story problems. Depending on the level of the children, have children mix operations and/or work on number families. After they have devised their solutions to different problems, discuss how and why they acted out the problem as they did. When groups present alternate approaches, talk about how it's possible that one problem can be solved in more than one way.

MOVING RIGHT ALONG: Assessment

While students are solving problems, ask questions. Their answers may provide insights into how they discover solutions for themselves and their ability to work with basic math facts. Check for their interpretations of given information. Look for their understanding of the results as well as the correctness of the process being used.

TAKING IT FURTHER: Extensions

✪ After students have gained some experience acting out story problems, provide them with a target value. Ask them to act out stories that have that value as the final answer. Ask: *How did you determine which numbers to put in the stories?* Invite them to explain how they solved the problem. Look for whether they chose one value and then determined the other value that would make the story work out correctly or whether they knew two numbers as facts for the target values.

usical Fraction Sheets

STEPPING UP: The Math Behind the Movement

Try musical chairs with a twist! When the music stops, instead of sitting on chairs, students stand on folded sheets. It's a fun and engaging way for young children to explore the idea of a denominator and halving. Children work to fit all the group members on a folded bedsheet of ever-decreasing area and learn—that fractions are part of a whole, and that as long as they are equal it doesn't matter what the parts look like.

JUMPING IN: The Activity

Before you begin, choose energetic music conducive to brisk, vigorous walking or marching. *The Lion King* soundtrack or John Philip Sousa marches work well for this activity.

Divide your class into groups of five to eight students. Provide each group with a bedsheet and have them lay the sheet flat on the floor. Explain that Musical Fraction Sheets is similar to the traditional game musical chairs.

When your students are ready, ask them to:

1. Line up around the perimeter of the sheet and listen for the music to play.

2. Walk around the sheet as the music plays.

3. Stand on the sheet when they hear the music stop, making sure everyone's feet are on the sheet.

4. Congratulate your students on the successful completion of the task. Then ask them to fold the sheet in half. Try not to give hints during the folding process. Children will develop their own ways of folding the sheet in half, making long rectangles or square folds, for example.

5. Repeat the steps above several times. Each time you stop the music, ask everyone to find a spot. Then have children fold the folded sheet in half again. Discuss ways in which students can help each other to stay on the sheet. They may suggest

Math Skills and Concepts
fractions—denominators and
  halving
problem solving
communication

Grouping
small groups

Movement
locomotor—walking
combined movement

Materials
◆ twin-size cloth sheets or
  vinyl tablecloths
◆ music

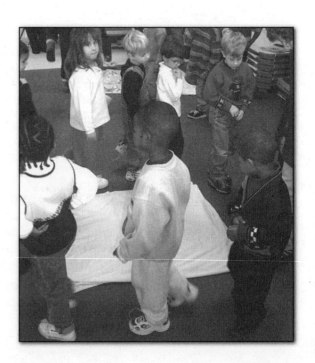

holding onto each other, using one foot to stand on the sheet and holding the other in the air, and so on.

When groups cannot stay on their sheet anymore, discuss what happened. Ask: *How did the area become too small for everyone in the group to fit?* Discuss how each group folded its sheet. Ask: *How did some groups fold their sheets in half in ways that were different from another group's method?* Then invite students to share their strategies for helping each other stay on the sheet.

MOVING RIGHT ALONG: Assessment

As they work together, listen to the children's discussions about how to fold the sheet and help one another stay on its surface. Consider using the first extension activity that follows as a way of further assessing student understanding.

TAKING IT FURTHER: Extensions

✪ Have students repeat the same steps they followed in their small group, only this time have them individually fold a piece of paper instead of a sheet. Folding the paper each time helps children see that the part of the sheet they had to stand on became smaller and smaller. It went from 1/2 to 1/4 to 1/8 and so on. You can take the fraction lesson even further by asking: *After folding the paper several times, how many squares or rectangles do you end up with?*

✪ Divide the class into pairs of students. Have children decide on various ways to fold a paper into three equal parts. Ask children to explain to their partners the steps they followed to do so.

umbo

STEPPING UP: The Math Behind the Movement

This toe-tapping activity has children singing along to the familiar tune "Bingo." Only this time the dog's name is Numbo and the song helps children learn about patterns. "Numbo," like "Bingo," has students say one less letter at each chorus. By following this "subtract one letter" rule, children explore related patterns. They also develop spatial sense as they use their bodies to form letter shapes.

JUMPING IN: The Activity

Discuss the song "Bingo." Ask: *What did you do in place of each letter as you sang each chorus?* Explain that this activity is called Numbo, named for an imaginary dog that likes numbers. Tell your students they will each be making letters with their individual bodies in place of the letters in Numbo's name. As a group, decide on ways to make the five letters with their bodies. Then have your students:

1. Stand in a circle facing the same direction.

2. Walk, skip, or gallop around the circle while singing "Numbo" to the tune of "Bingo." Have them sing it through once, saying all five letters.

3. Sing the song again, but leave off the N. In its place, have students use their bodies to make a shape to represent N.

4. Repeat the song six times until all letters (U, M, B, O) are formed using their bodies instead of their voices.

MOVING RIGHT ALONG: Assessment

Look for each child's developing spatial-sense ability by checking whether the pattern is followed and the body forms used to make the letters N, U, M, B, and O make sense.

TAKING IT FURTHER: Extensions

✪ Ask students to suggest other five-letter names for Numbo the dog. Sing about them to the tune of "Bingo."

Math Skills and Concepts
patterns
spatial sense
representation

Grouping
whole class

Movement
locomotor—dancing,
  skipping, etc.
perceptual skills

Materials
◆ none

Create-a-Dance

STEPPING UP: The Math Behind the Movement

Create-a-Dance gives students opportunities to design their own dance routine, which is a pattern of movements. Through this concrete learning experience, they strengthen their understanding of the concept and learn to recognize patterns in different modalities.

JUMPING IN: The Activity

Explain that each student will design his or her own dance pattern. You may want to model a simple AAB pattern for students, for example: spin, spin, flap both arms. As a class:

1. Discuss familiar patterns, such as ABA or ABC.

2. Tell children that we can create patterns in different ways. For instance, in dancing we follow patterns of body movements.

3. Brainstorm movements that can be used easily in a dance.

4. Ask students to create their own personal pattern. For example, an ABC pattern could be: jump, step, twirl.

5. Invite some students to show their dance patterns and describe what strategies they used to follow it.

6. Create and record a system of letters, symbols, stamps, or stickers for recording a few patterns. For example, SFSF could stand for the pattern: spin, flap, spin, flap.

MOVING RIGHT ALONG: Assessment

Compare students' dance patterns with their ability to record the pattern symbolically. Consider documenting learning by videotaping the class's dance routines.

TAKING IT FURTHER: Extensions

✪ Take learning a step further by discussing pattern similarities. Ask: *What is another way we've learned to write patterns like step, twirl, step, twirl and hop, clap, hop, clap?* (ABAB)

Math Skills and Concepts
patterning
translating from one
    representation to another
communication
representation

Grouping
whole class

Movement
locomotor—dancing,
    jumping, etc.
physical fitness—flexibility
creative movement

Materials
◆ recording materials (paper and pencils)

Anatomy Patterns

STEPPING UP: The Math Behind the Movement

Bring giggles into math learning by creating repeated patterns with everything from elbows to toes! Start with patterns of varying difficulty levels, such as ABAB, ABBABB, and ABCCABCC, to help lay the foundation of your students' pattern learning. As they develop their skills, young learners can use what they know about a pattern to determine what comes next. Explain: *Since I just did B, now I need another B, and then it's back to A.* Not only does learning simple repeated patterns help to set students on the road to successfully following and creating simple set-sequence patterns, it helps set the groundwork for their learning of growing patterns, such as arithmetic sequences.

JUMPING IN: The Activity

To help your students follow simple repeated patterns, begin this activity by modeling what you expect them to do. You might show an ABAB card, for example, and show them a pattern by pointing with your index finger to your elbow, chin, elbow, and chin. Invite them to follow and then repeat your example. When your students are ready, divide your class into small groups.

1. One child, the Presenter, draws a card and builds that pattern once or twice by pointing to various limbs, facial features, and extremities. For example, if a card has the pattern ABCABC, a student might point to his or her nose, knee, shoulder, nose, knee, and shoulder.

2. The other children follow the same pattern, pointing to their noses, knees, and shoulders—following the pattern's order and number of repetitions.

3. Take this lesson one step further by inviting a Presenter in each group to write a pattern on a blank card and then share it with his or her group. Many students will love this opportunity to teach their peers what they know about patterns. Alternate Presenters, providing each member of your class with the opportunity to create a repeated pattern.

Math Skills and Concepts
creating, following, and
   building patterns
problem solving
communication
making connections

Grouping
whole class
small groups

Movement
non-locomotor—stretching,
   reaching, coordination
perceptual skills

Materials
◆ markers
◆ several decks of index cards
   with repeated patterns
   printed on them (such as
   ABBA, ABCABC, and ABAB)

MOVING RIGHT ALONG: Assessment

Check for understanding of repeated patterns by observing your students as they follow a pattern and direct their peers. If your students have had an opportunity to record their original patterns on paper, review their work.

TAKING IT FURTHER: Extensions

✪ Add fun and flavor by playing music with a strong beat while your students follow a pattern. Take learning a step further by inviting your students to build growing patterns. For example, a Presenter could point to an elbow once, mouth twice, and an ear three times. Each child in the group then responds by repeating the pattern. A second Presenter adds a fourth repetition, a third Presenter adds a fifth, and so on. For added fun, teach your class anatomical terms or invite students to say the first letter of each extremity as they create and follow patterns.

TIP!

Instead of having young learners write their patterns, invite them to state their patterns aloud. The skill of transferring the patterns they created with their bodies (a concrete activity) to writing a repeated pattern of letters (an abstract concept represented with letters) may be a daunting task for some students.

Pitter-Patter Poems

STEPPING UP: The Math Behind the Movement

Use poetry, with its playful rhymes and rhythms, as a springboard for teaching patterns. Using simple body movements to express the patterns they encounter in poetry, students learn to recognize repeated word patterns. In addition, as children respond to written patterns with body movements, they learn a key math concept—that patterns may be translated from one representational form to another.

JUMPING IN: The Activity

Before you begin, choose a poem with a pattern or repeating rhyme, such as Shel Silverstein's "Boa Constrictor" from *Where the Sidewalk Ends*. Or select an easy-to-read book, such as Joy Cowley's *Mr. Grump Grump* (available as a Big Book). Print the words to your selection on chart paper so children have a visual representation of the piece. Explain to students that they will be showing the patterns they hear by moving their bodies. Ask students to sit side by side in a circle on the floor. When they're ready for the activity:

1. Read the poem several times, so children are well acquainted and comfortable with the words in it.

Math Skills and Concepts
categorizing
problem solving
communication
representation

Grouping
four groups

Movement
locomotor—hopping,
  crawling, etc.
physical fitness—agility

Materials
◆ poem
◆ many small objects of
  different colors and shapes
◆ masking tape

2. Discuss the poem. Help children identify and recognize its repeating pattern.

3. Invite them to think of different ways they could move, such as clapping their hands overhead or behind their backs.

4. Divide the class into two groups. Tell them that the groups will take turns being Presenters and Observers. Have the first group of Presenters show its movements as you read the poem aloud. Then have the other half of the class, the Observers, look at how well the Presenters showed the poem's pattern with their body movements.

5. Ask the groups to switch roles, giving the Presenters an opportunity to be Observers and vice versa.

MOVING RIGHT ALONG: Assessment

Observe children as they take on the roles of Presenters and Observers. Look for each student to demonstrate a developing understanding of patterns by moving his or her body according to the poem's repeated patterns. Additionally, invite students to help each other follow patterns. Look for students who are able to detect another student's inability to follow a pattern, as well as his or her own ability to model or offer advice about following patterns.

TAKING IT FURTHER: Extensions

✪ Assign Pitter-Patter Poems homework! Ask students to bring a poem with repeating patterns from home. Encourage them to look with their families for poems in favorite books or think of jump-rope jingles. Have children make up movements that correspond to their poems' patterns.

✪ Make a collection of the patterned poems for your class to read and to move to. Have the child who brought the poem present the movement pattern he or she has created.

✪ Invite older children to choose pattern-packed poems from poetry collections you've placed in the classroom library. Have students copy a poem on chart paper, create new movements, and share their pattern with partners. Each child needs to teach the movement pattern to his or her partner and then switch roles.

Skip Relay

STEPPING UP: The Math Behind the Movement

In Skip Relay, children learn number patterns through movement. Following the skip-counting rule that builds the pattern, they move their bodies and count aloud. For example, if the pattern is "count by 2s," each child hops twice. Then, he or she says the number "2" and hops twice, says the number "4" and hops two times, says the number "6" and hops two times, and so on. It's patterning and fun rolled into one!

JUMPING IN: The Activity

At opposite ends of the classroom, place lengths of masking tape on the floor. These will serve as both start and finish lines.

Divide the class into teams of four students. Describe to the class how the relay works: A student from each team will skip count and move from the starting line to the finish line. As a class, decide on the movements children will use in the activity, such as: skips, hops, and giant steps. Then determine which skip-counting pattern the class will use. For example, will the class be counting by 2s or 5s?

Explain that half of each team will begin the relay from the opposite end of the classroom. At opposite relay lines, two members from each team stand single file and face their teammates at the other end of the room. Then the relay is ready to begin.

1. The first student from each team moves (skips, jumps, or hops) toward the finish line. There the two other team members are waiting to take a turn.

2. He or she needs to say the number pattern after making the appropriate number of movements. For example, a child skip counting by 2 might: hop, hop a second time, then say "2," hop the third time, hop a fourth time and say "4," and so on until he or she reaches the other relay line.

3. When that child reaches the finish line, he or she needs to touch the next participating member's hand. That team member starts his leg of the relay by repeating the same

Math Skills and Concepts
counting
patterning
communication
making connections
representation

Grouping
whole class
small groups

Movement
locomotor—skipping, hopping
  crawling, etc.

Materials
◆ masking tape
◆ markers
◆ several decks of index cards with repeated patterns printed on them (such as ABBA, ABCABC, and ABAB)

action as the previous player, skip counting as he or she performs each movement.

The relay continues until each team member has completed his or her leg of the relay. After all students have participated, another pattern and/or another movement can be performed to a skip-count pattern.

MOVING RIGHT ALONG: Assessment

Focus on one group of children at a time. Check each student's ability to vebalize the number pattern. Observe their movements. Look for each student's ability to make the correct number of movements as he or she verbalizes the number pattern.

TAKING IT FURTHER: Extensions

✪ Have students continue skip counting, building on the pattern the previous team member used. For example, if a child reaches the finish line after having counted and done the movements for the 2 pattern (2, 4, 6), then the next team member needs to build the pattern to larger values (8, 10, 12).

✪ You might also invite children to skip count backward. Have students return to the line where they started the relay instead of going to the finish line. Tell students to use a different movement or use the same movement but in reverse as they follow a pattern of subtracting by two (6, 4, 2).

Playing Out Problems

STEPPING UP: The Math Behind the Movement

By actually being part of a math problem, students gain experience with variables and the problem-solving process. They physically and mentally work through each part of the problem, practicing important math skills, including: identifying goals and given information, developing goal-reaching strategies, dealing with unexpected obstacles, and reflecting on the reasonableness of their solution and the process they used to obtain to that answer. Since problems in this activity can have more than one correct answer, children gain experience with variables without being overwhelmed by symbolism or a need to find correct answers.

JUMPING IN: The Activity

Model the problem-solving process by first working through one or two questions with the whole class. Use only a few students to act out the problem while the rest of the class observes.

Divide the class into small groups. Read aloud one word problem from the list below. Have each group of students:

1. Discuss what the problem is about.

2. Decide how to use their bodies to work toward solving the problem.

3. Become the values, acting out the problem step by step.

4. Identify an answer.

Invite the groups to share their answers with the class. Since the word problems are designed to have more than one correct answer, this class discussion is an important way for students to learn that other groups may have different correct answers and that their methods make sense.

Repeat the process with a new problem. Here are a few to get started:

Behind the Fence A farmer put several animals in a pen. Some were chickens and others were pigs. The farmer

Math Skills and Concepts
variables
problem solving
reasoning
communication

Grouping
group sizes will vary

Movement
combined movement

Materials
◆ none

wondered how many animals were in the pen. When he looked under the fence he saw 12 feet. How many chickens and how many pigs were in the pen? (If there are extra actors they can be the farmer's helpers.)

Ride on the Playground A group of children decided to meet on the playground after school to do some riding. Some brought scooters and the others brought tricycles. Suddenly, one of the kids exclaimed, "Wow! There sure are a lot of wheels here. I counted 18 wheels!" How many tricycles were on the playground? How many scooters?

Animal Dance The gym teacher announces that your class is going to learn a new dance. It's going to include moving your bodies like three different kinds of animals. Some children will crab-walk, others will stand on one leg like a flamingo, and the rest will jump like kangaroos. To make the dance really exciting, each dancer gets to wear special animal shoes. They look like the animal's feet the children are portraying in the dance. As you prepare to go into the gym, you notice 12 of these neat animal shoes in a row. How many of each animal are participating in your class's dance?

Note: The values in these problems were chosen to allow for several right answers by using common multiples. If you would like to create word problems that relate to what your class is currently studying, be sure to vary the values depending on group size and your students' developing skills.

MOVING RIGHT ALONG: Assessment

Evaluate your students' explanations during the class discussions. Did they realize they tried a variety of strategies to solve the problem? Look for evidence that students based their choices on sound reasoning.

TAKING IT FURTHER: Extensions

✪ Invite students to illustrate each word problem. Look for their developing ability to transfer the concrete experience to the representational, visual format. This extension, which can be used as an assessment tool, provides an opportunity to discuss how students determined answers. Provide younger students with cutouts of the word-problem characters. Or, provide manipulatives they can use in retelling how they solved the word problem.

ibbon Dance

STEPPING UP: The Math Behind the Movement

Increase your students' math vocabulary by demonstrating the meanings of spatial and geometric words with swirling and twirling streamers! By manipulating streamers, children show their grasp of key concepts such as near, far; up, down; under, over; and shapes such as triangles, squares, and circles. What's more, students are encouraged to talk about what they're doing as they're doing it. In this way, children express their understanding through both word and action.

JUMPING IN: The Activity

Before you begin, select dancing music. Lively music with varying tempos works best for this activity.

Explain that, as they dance to music, the class is going to use streamers to show the meanings of certain words. First you'll say a word. Then children will illustrate its meaning by moving the streamers in different ways. For example: If you say the word *fast*, a child might dance his or her streamers back and forth quickly to show the meaning of the word. When the class is ready:

1. Give each child one or more streamers.

2. Play music and say a word from the list below.

3. Observe students' streamer movements.

4. Ask several students to describe their actions. For example, a child waving the streamers above his or her head may describe the action by saying, "The streamer is *above* my head."

5. Periodically stop the music. Take a few minutes to encourage children to explain how they demonstrated a particular word's meaning.

6. Invite students to take turns being the Caller. Whisper a word to the Caller, then invite the Caller to say the word aloud as students show its meaning.

Math Skills and Concepts
spatial vocabulary
communication
representation

Grouping
whole class

Movement
using manipulatives
locomotor—dancing, etc.
non-locomotor—stretching,
    swaying, etc.

Materials
◆ music
◆ streamers (crepe paper, scarves, or ribbons)

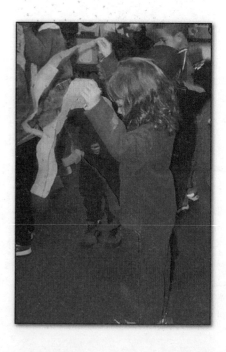

Words, emotions, and concepts to explore might include:
    distance (far, near)
    emotions and moods (happy, sad, angry, quiet, joy)
    speed (fast, slow)
    space (behind, between, in front, in back, inside, outside)
    size (small, medium, big, bigger, biggest)
    order (first, next, last)
    directionality (up, down, behind, under, over, left, right,
      backward, forward, around)
    modes (sideways, in the middle, backward)
    shapes (circle, square, triangle, line, straight)

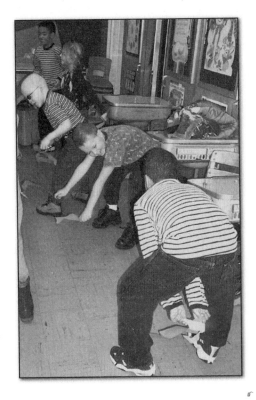

MOVING RIGHT ALONG: **Assessment**

Observe children's responses to different words. Are they
illustrating the word's meaning? Or are they imitating other
students' actions? Look for each student's ability to demonstrate
understanding of a particular word or concept through action
and verbal description. Consider using the word list above
as a checklist.

TAKING IT FURTHER: **Extensions**

✪ Divide the class into small groups. Have each group
  demonstrate the meanings of several words using their
  bodies, without streamers. The following words work well
  for this activity: larger, smaller, first, second, big, and little.
  Ask one child to give a description of the word and invite
  other children to act out the description. Or ask one child
  to act out the word while the other group members describe
  its meaning in as many ways as they can.

Bend-a-Bit Shape Making

STEPPING UP: The Math Behind the Movement

Bend-a-Bit Shape Making is an activity that begins with students discussing the attributes of geometric shapes, then moves to problem-solving ways to arrange their bodies to form these shapes. Working together, children make circles, squares, triangles, rectangles, and so on. In the process, they strengthen their understanding of various shapes' attributes. For example, a group of four students may arrange their bodies in a square, demonstrating that they've learned that a square is made of four sides of equal lengths.

JUMPING IN: The Activity

Before you begin, find a classroom area in which students have room to move their bodies, or use an empty playground or a quiet hallway. Ask your students to name some of the shapes they know.

Explain that groups of children will be arranging their bodies to form shapes. Every member of the group needs to participate in building the shape with at least one part of his or her body. Divide the class into three to four groups of children. When they are ready, tell the class which shape to make. Ask each group of children to:

1. Visualize the shape.

2. Discuss within the group how to position their bodies to form it.

3. Create the shapes with their bodies.

4. Observe how other groups show the same shape.

As a class, discuss the similarities and differences between the structures. Ask: *Is there another way a group could have made that shape?* Invite students to try constructing shapes with their whole bodies, and then with just limbs. Discuss how they determine that they have formed a shape correctly.

Repeat the process several times, having groups create different types of shapes, both curved and straight-sided.

Math Skills and Concepts
spatial awareness
problem solving
communication
representation

Grouping
groups of four to five

Movement
non-locomotor—pushing, curling, etc.
combined movement
creative movement

Materials
◆ none

MOVING RIGHT ALONG: Assessment

As students try to meet the challenge of using each group member's body in forming a shape, try to gain insights into their understanding. For example: Five students attempting to create a square may end up discussing the fact that the shape only needs four children to show the equal length of the four sides. As a result, they may place group members in a way that utilizes all the children to form the square.

Invite a parent to take photos of the class forming shapes with their bodies. Use the photos to make a class display. Encourage students to examine the photos and compare how the same shape can be expressed in different ways.

TAKING IT FURTHER: Extensions

✪ Have students independently make shapes such as a circle—where some may use their fingers and others use their arms. Challenge the groups to see if each member can find a different way to represent the named shape.

✪ Create groups so that each one has a different number of members. For example: group one has 3 members, group two has 5 members, group three has 4 members, and group four has 6 members. Then as students look at the shapes that different groups make, the discussion should be rich in comparisons.

iamond Dance

STEPPING UP: **The Math Behind the Movement**

As they play Diamond Dance, a form of follow the leader, children develop ability to form and recognize shapes. They develop spatial sense in the process of copying the movements of their leader and positioning their bodies to form shapes.

JUMPING IN: **The Activity**

Before you begin, find an area in the room where children will have plenty of space to move. Select music with gentle rhythms. (Music by Enya works well for this activity.)

Explain to students that they'll be doing an activity similar to follow the leader. In Diamond Dance, students create dancing diamond shapes to music. Divide the class into groups of approximately four students. When the class is ready:

1. Ask groups to stand forming the diamond's shape. Each member of the group represents a vertex.

2. Have students face the same direction, toward the front of the classroom. If a group has five members, have one child stand in the middle of the diamond.

3. Play the music.

4. Tell the child at the front of each diamond that he or she is the group's leader for the next few moments. As the child moves his or her arms, hands, and upper body to the music, other students in the diamond copy his or her actions. As a result, each group of children does a different kind of a diamond dance. Younger children may need to be reminded to follow the leader in their own group's diamond.

Math Skills and Concepts
geometry
spatial sense
communication
making connections
representation

Grouping
small groups of four to five

Movement
perceptual skills
combined movement
creative movement

Materials
◆ slow music

5. Ask students to turn and face another direction, such as toward the wall with the clock or toward the windows. With the new arrangement, the child in the front of the diamond becomes the leader. The group follows his or her actions.

6. Repeat the process at least three times, giving each child in the group an opportunity to be the leader and an opportunity to develop his or her own unique movements. If a group has a child in the middle of the diamond, ask that child to switch places with a classmate who has already been a leader.

After the activity, discuss the experience. Ask: *When you turned your bodies to make a new diamond, what happened to the diamond shape? In what ways was it difficult or easy to keep the diamond shape? How is the experience of being a leader different from being a follower?*

MOVING RIGHT ALONG: Assessment

Observe students as they copy the movement of their leader. Is changing direction a problem? Are some movements difficult to copy? When a child becomes the leader, is he or she able to create distinctive body movements?

TAKING IT FURTHER: Extensions

☼ Encourage students to brainstorm objects in their community's environment that have a diamond shape. Record the list on chart paper. (Examples might include: signs, windows, sidewalk mosaics, and brickwork.) Use the list as inspiration for another round of Diamond Dance.

Mystery Shapes

STEPPING UP: The Math Behind the Movement

Though they are familiar with shapes, young children need to learn the attributes that differentiate a square from a rectangle, a rectangle from a triangle, and so on. Mystery Shapes places the study of shapes in the fun and unfamiliar setting of sound. It's an activity that asks students to identify shapes based on the sounds they hear. For example, if a teacher draws a circle in the air with a plastic bag, children would hear just one starting and one ending sound. If a teacher drew a polygon, students would hear stopping and starting sounds for each line segment.

JUMPING IN: The Activity

Before you begin, explain that students will be listening to the sounds of shapes being drawn in the air. Show the plastic bag. Invite students to discuss how they would know what you've drawn if their eyes are closed. Provide an example of what is meant by listening to shapes. In the air, slowly draw a simple closed shape such as a square or a triangle. Be sure to accentuate the starting and stopping of each side (the vertices). Ask students to describe the sounds they heard. If they heard the sounds "swoosh, swoosh, swoosh," that would indicate that the shape drawn was a triangle. When the class is ready, have students:

1. Close their eyes and listen as you make a shape.

2. Tell what mystery shape they think was drawn.

3. Provide support for their guesses based on the number of sounds they heard and the length of the sounds. For example, a child might say, "I heard you make four sounds, all in a row. I think you made a square."

4. Close their eyes and listen as you make the shape again. Ask: *Are these the sounds you heard? Did I make a square?*

Give each of your students his or her personal plastic bag. After the class has gone through the

Math Skills and Concepts
spatial awareness
identification
reasoning
communication
representation

Grouping
whole class
small groups

Movement
non-locomotor—stretching, swaying, reaching, etc.

Materials
◆ plastic grocery bags

process of identifying a shape based on the sounds heard, ask your students to make the same shape. Encourage them to listen to the sounds they make as they draw that shape.

MOVING RIGHT ALONG: Assessment

Check each student's ability to identify shapes. Can they provide support for their answers? Is each child able to draw the shapes with his or her own plastic bag?

TAKING IT FURTHER: Extensions

✪ Choose a student to be the class shape-maker. Have the class repeat the same process as above, with children listening, guessing the mystery shape, and supporting their guesses.

✪ Try having students make representations of shapes with other materials. Use soft objects that they manipulate, such as: ribbon, yarn, modeling clay, and so forth. Have older students draw shapes with crayons.

Safety Tip!

Supervise children closely during this activity, as plastic bags are a potential choking hazard. For younger children, try using lengths of plastic streamers for a similar effect.

liding Along

STEPPING UP: The Math Behind the Movement

Sliding Along introduces students to the ways in which three-dimensional objects move through space. First, children trace a classmate's body to create an outline of a person. Then they're challenged to visualize how objects move in terms of transformations. A *transformation* is when an object changes its location, but its shape and size remain the same. In this activity, children explore how objects (people) slide through space without changing direction, spin or rotate around a point, and flip over a line (real or imagined).

JUMPING IN: The Activity

Before you begin, explain that the class will work together as detectives to figure out what transformation a body outline would have to make to move to a certain place. Describe how shapes move in three ways: like arrows going in one direction, like tops spinning, and like gymnasts doing somersaults. For younger children, the word *transformation* is a mouthful. Invite them to use familiar words like *slide, spin,* and *flip* to describe the ways in which shapes move. When the class is ready:

1. Have a child lay down and hold his or her body in an asymmetrical position. Trace a his or her body outline on a piece of bulletin-board paper.

2. Lay another sheet of paper on top of the outline and trace it, making two identical tracings.

3. Place the two body tracings on top of each other.

4. Ask all but two students to turn their backs or close their eyes.

5. Have the two remaining students move one of the outlines to a new spot on the floor using one transformation or several. For example: If children slide the outline forward several feet, they've used one transformation. If they move the outline forward and

Math Skills and Concepts
transformation
spatial awareness
problem solving
reasoning
communication

Grouping
whole class

Movement
using manipulatives
perceptual skills

Materials
◆ bulletin-board paper
◆ markers

turn it sideways, they've used two different transformations. If children move the outline forward a few feet, turn it sideways, and flip it upside down, they've used all three transformations.

6. Invite the rest of the class to examine and talk about the outlines. Ask questions to guide their problem solving, such as: *How would the outline need to move to have gotten to its new position? What would we need to do to make the two outlines match up? Would the outline need to change directions? Flip flop? Is there more than one way to solve this mystery?*

7. Discuss your detectives' observations and conclusions.

8. Repeat the activity several times.

MOVING RIGHT ALONG: Assessment

Listen to students' discussions as they problem-solve, taking special note of their descriptions of what happened. Look for their ability to provide evidence as to how many transformations the body shape needed to take to move to its new location.

TAKING IT FURTHER: Extensions

✪ Try teaching this activity with live people! Place the children in two locations in the classroom. Ask students to figure out which transformations are needed to move one child to the other's location. Younger children may have more success learning with this variation of the Sliding Along activity.

We Can Be . . .

STEPPING UP: The Math Behind the Movement

Turn students into shape engineers! In We Can Be . . . , students work together to create human representations of common objects in their environment, such as cars, tables, airplanes, and telephones. They use what they know about shapes to decide how to arrange their bodies and show the objects' functions.

JUMPING IN: The Activity

Before you begin, invite students to look at some familiar objects around the classroom. Ask children to name the shape and say how the object works. For example, a table might look like a square with four legs. The four legs keep the flat surface of the table from falling down when you're using it. When students are ready:

1. Invite volunteers to name an object. Younger students may find it helpful to be told where they should look for the object, such as in a desk drawer, a lunch box, or a knapsack.

2. Ask them to use their bodies to form the various parts of the object. For example, if the children are making a car, some students will be wheels, some will be head-lights, some will be doors, and so on.

Math Skills and Concepts
spatial reasoning
identifying attributes
problem solving
reasoning
communication
representation

Grouping
whole class

Movement
non-locomotor—swinging, curling, etc.
combined movement

Materials
◆ none

3. Have students explain what each part of their object does and why it's shaped the way it is. For example, if they are the wheels on a car, the children may say, "Wheels are round so they can roll."

MOVING RIGHT ALONG: Assessment

Observe children's actions. Listen to their descriptions of various object parts and their function. Have children identified the object's shape and its related parts? Have they positioned their bodies in ways that represent the object's function?

TAKING IT FURTHER: Extensions

✪ Invite students to become inventors. Ask questions that guide students in their problem-solving process, such as: *How could we change the shape of this stapler in ways that would help people?* When asked such a question, students may decide to add round wheels to make the stapler move across a desk easily.

rans-Dance

STEPPING UP: The Math Behind the Movement

In a virtual square dance, called a Trans-Dance, children learn about the ways objects move through space: translating (sliding) and rotating (spinning). This activity invites children to dance with partners using slides and spins.

JUMPING IN: The Activity

Before you begin, explain to students that you will give them directions using words, such as *forward, spin,* and *backward*. Discuss what each word means.

Divide the class into groups of four children each. Have them arrange themselves in pairs that face each other. Tell students that either the person they are facing is their partner, or the person who is beside them is their partner. Who their partner is depends on which dance movement is specified.

Math Skills and Concepts
spatial awareness
geometric operations
reasoning
representation

Grouping
small groups of four

Movement
locomotor—sliding,
   spinning, etc.

Materials
◆ none

Have students start with the slide-dance movements below:

1. Tell students that their partner is the child standing next to them.

2. For the first dance movement, have partners slide two steps to the right. (For younger students, who may not know their left from their right, give simple directions such as: "If you're facing the clock, slide toward the door. If you're facing the flag, slide toward the windows.")

Ask: *If you needed to move back to where you started, how many sliding steps would you need to take?*

3. In the second dance movement, have partners slide two steps forward.

Ask: *How do you move back to where you started? How many slides would you need to make?*

4. In the third dance movement, have the pairs slide two steps left.

Ask: *How do your new positions compare with where you were when we began? What would you need to do to return to your original positions?*

5. Encourage students to discuss different solutions to the problem, using only sliding steps. Tell them that in order to return to their original positions, they cannot turn around (spin) and they cannot run into one another. Every student must make the same number of slides in the same direction.

When your students are ready, invite them to add spin movements. For example, you might give the following directions: *Your partner is the person across from you. Turn around so you and your partner are back to back. Each of you, move two sliding steps forward.* In order to move back to their original positions, students would need to identify two kinds of movements—the slides they used going forward and the spin they used turning around. Have students reverse their movements and see what happens.

MOVING RIGHT ALONG: Assessment

Observe students as they follow your directions. Talk with individual students to gain insights about their understanding of how objects move. Are they able to describe how to return to their original positions? Do they understand the difference between slides and spins?

TAKING IT FURTHER: Extensions

✪ Invite small groups of children to put slides and spins together in a dance. Have children record their dances on paper, using symbols and illustrations.

✪ Invite each group to show its dance to the class. First have them share the way they recorded their dance and tell how the symbols and pictures give them clues about how to move. Then have them demonstrate their dance. Set the dances to music.

ing Around

STEPPING UP: **The Math Behind the Movement**

Invite young children to measure perimeter and circumference using non-standard units of measurement. This Ring Around activity and the class discussion that follows it draw students' attention to issues of accuracy and the value of standard units of measure.

JUMPING IN: **The Activity**

As a class, create a list of several items to measure, such as tables, desks, cups, pencils, books, a person, or the room.

Divide the class into groups. Have the children in each group:

1. Determine a way to measure the distance around various objects. They may use their bodies or parts of their bodies, such as: finger length, arm span, or body width.

2. Measure each item on the list.

3. Record their measurements and what part of their body they used to measure.

As a class, discuss the units of measure and the results. Encourage children to make comparisons between different measuring units (parts of the body).

MOVING RIGHT ALONG: **Assessment**

Initially, ask children to explain why they chose a particular item as a measuring tool. Then observe them measuring classroom items. Are they striving for accuracy? Are they trying to effectively use their bodies and one another as measuring tools? Examine the measurement records. Look for insight into their ability to record measurement data.

TAKING IT FURTHER: **Extensions**

✪ Have children compare their group's measurements with those of other groups. Ask: *Why were there differences in each group's results?* Invite students to offer possible explanations.

Math Skills and Concepts
estimation
gathering data
using nonstandard units of measurement
reasoning
communication
representation

Grouping
whole class
small groups of four to five

Movement
non-locomotor—reaching, stretching, etc.
physical fitness—flexibility

Materials
◆ various objects to measure
◆ recording materials (paper and pencils)

ocoon

STEPPING UP: The Math Behind the Movement

Help young learners practice their developing skills of measuring and estimating with a standard household item—toilet tissue! This activity begins with your students taking an important first step in the learning process, developing a basis for their estimates. Most of us find it much easier to estimate the length of a long object when we have a concrete sense of the length of a shorter object. (Isn't it easier to estimate how long your leg is when you know how long your thigh is?) In measuring to see how close their own estimations are, your students will also gain practice skip counting by bigger numbers (5s or 10s, for example), learning to collect and record data in a systematic manner, and using their results to make comparisons.

JUMPING IN: The Activity

Begin by asking your students what they know about measuring and estimating, challenging them to think about the estimating process.

1. Show children a roll of toilet tissue and ask: *How much toilet tissue would it take to cover the length of your arm?* As a class, cover one person's arm, unwrap it, and count the number of sheets used. Then ask how many sheets they would need to wrap a whole person up to the shoulders! Expect all types of numbers from 10 to 200 from your young learners. Accept each suggestion. In fact, record them so you can revisit their estimates at the conclusion of the activity.

2. Divide the class into groups of four, so each member of each group has a job (Caterpillar, Wrapper, Measurer, and Recorder). Note: Each member of the class will have an assigned role, but it is important for all students to experience the math concepts explored in each role. Consider repeating the activity several times so that each child has a chance to take each job.

Math Skills and Concepts
linear measurement
gathering data
estimation
communication
representation
reasoning and proof

Grouping
whole class, then groups of four to five

Movement
non-locomotor—stretching, grasping, coordination

Materials
- rolls of strong toilet tissue (one per group)
- recording materials (paper and pencils)
- camera (optional)

Safety Tip!
The Caterpillar should hold his or her arms to his or her sides, so he or she does not become bound too tightly or find standing difficult. Some Caterpillars may prefer to lay on the floor during the cocooning process.

3. Have each group choose one member to be wrapped with toilet tissue (the Caterpillar). The Wrapper should start with the feet (legs together) and wrap the Caterpillar from toes to shoulders.

4. Ask the Measurer for each group to carefully unwrap the Caterpillar, folding the tissue as they unwrap.

5. Tell the Measurer for each group to start counting how many sheets of toilet tissue were used and to share this data with the Recorder, who then writes and tallies the numbers for the group. To keep this part of the activity from becoming messy, encourage groups to measure their tissue in separate corners of the classroom where they'll have ample space to spread out.

6. Observe students' experiences with measuring as they embark on counting each square of toilet tissue. Invite them to think about ways they could speed up the counting and measuring process and record the results.

7. Finally, come together as a class to share each group's results. Invite the Recorder from each group to share the strategies the group used to count and record quickly. Discuss various methods of gathering and recording information.

8. Compare students' results with their original estimates. Then invite your students to share their reactions and conclusions.

MOVING RIGHT ALONG: Assessment

Pay close attention to the way that your students explain their estimates and how they suggest carrying out the measuring. Divide the work among the children in each group, since those who are actively involved throughout the experience gain the most in terms of their conceptual understanding.

TAKING IT FURTHER: Extensions

✪ Instead of a cocoon, make a mummy! Invite students to wrap a classmate from toes to shoulders. Take this activity a step further by asking how the results would differ if the limbs (legs and arms) were wrapped separately. Or invite students to devise a different way to measure how much tissue was used. Ask: *Instead of measuring the length of tissue we need with squares of toilet tissue, what could we use?*

 alloping Giants

STEPPING UP: The Math Behind the Movement

One way to help students learn why people use standard units of measure is to give them hands-on experience in measuring without them. Galloping Giants offers students an opportunity to use the varying length of their gallop, or giant-sized stride, as a nonstandard unit of measure. Since each child's gallop is a different length, children will accurately find different answers to the same question of length.

JUMPING IN: The Activity

Begin this activity by sharing a tale that will be sure to capture your students' imaginations. Tell the story of a king and queen who needed to measure the distance between certain items in their enormous castle. One day the royal couple came upon a band of friendly giants. Thinking that the giants' big size made them perfect for the job of measuring long distances, the king and queen asked the giants for help. The giants happily agreed. What happened next in the story is for your students (the giants) to discover.

Ask the class to pretend the school or classroom is a castle. Each student (or giant!) counts how many giant gallops (or giant steps) it is from one place to another. For example, you might require students to measure the distance between the door and your desk, one classroom and another, or the cafeteria and the library.

1. After practicing a few gallops, students measure and record the assigned distances.

2. After measuring and recording several distances, examine the results as a class. Discuss what students noticed about the answers they found. Help focus the classroom discussion on possible reasons for different answers. Invite students to offer explanations and interpretations for the discrepancies. Ask: *Why aren't all the answers the same? Did some children need to use*

Math Skills and Concepts
using nonstandard units of
   measurement
counting
reasoning
communication

Grouping
groups of two

Movement
locomotor—galloping, or
   giant stepping

Materials
◆ recording materials (paper and pencils)

half-gallops in their measurements? Were all children's gallops the same length? Then discuss the ways in which students tried to ensure accuracy and some of the strategies they used to avoid making mistakes in counting.

3. Ask students to check their work. Because the length of a gallop's stride is difficult to maintain throughout the measuring process, students are likely to find different measurements the second time they measure. The idea that the length of a student's gallop may not be consistently the same length each time he or she measures is important for students to think about. To strengthen their understanding of units of measure, discuss how it could be that the same student, measuring with his or her own distinctive gallop, could find different answers.

MOVING RIGHT ALONG: Assessment

Have individual students describe and then demonstrate the process they used for measuring. Listen to their explanations to assess their growing understanding of units of measure.

TAKING IT FURTHER: Extensions

✪ Invite students to come up with a noncustomary standardized unit of measure that works better than the length of a gallop's stride. For example, some students may want to use a different movement. Some may want to use several students in the activity. Others may want to measure distance using wooden blocks laid end to end. Encourage ingenuity as students determine objects with which to measure. Then have them measure a specific distance. Discuss the results.

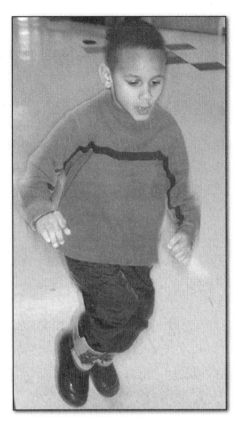

Am Fastest When . . .

STEPPING UP: The Math Behind the Movement

As children playfully hop or gallop from place to place, they increase their understanding of the concept of time. Through I Am Fastest When . . . children explore timing and the idea of faster, fastest, slower, and slowest in terms of distance traveled or in terms of numbers counted.

JUMPING IN: The Activity

Before you begin, lay down lengths of masking tape to serve as starting and finishing lines at either end of the work space. A playground, hallway, or gymnasium works well for this activity. Invite several students to demonstrate different movements, such as: crawling, hopping, crab walking, skipping, galloping, and so on. Tell children that they'll be performing those movements in this activity.

Explain that they are going to find out how long it takes for a child to move over a certain distance when he's skipping, galloping, and so forth. Ask your students to predict which way they will be fastest: Will it be hopping? crab walking? Invite children to offer reasons as support for their predictions. Record their responses. The class will revisit these predictions at the conclusion of the activity.

2 = 9 = A + 3 = 8 = 0 + 5 = 6 =

Math Skills and Concepts
estimation
time measurement
predicting
gathering data
reasoning
communication

Grouping
whole class
groups of two

Movement
locomotor—crawling, galloping, skipping, crab walking, etc.
physical fitness—agility

2 □ 3 △ 2 ▷ □ 8

Materials
◆ masking tape
◆ recording materials (paper and pencils)

Before starting, help children practice counting in seconds with the "one Mississippi, two Mississippi" technique. (They love it and it helps them count seconds with some accuracy.) Divide the class into groups of two. When ready, tell the class which method of movement to use and say, "Go!" Then:

1. Have one child move from one location to the other, such as across the room or down the hall from one marked spot to another, while the partner counts how long it takes.

2. Tell each team to record how many seconds it took for his or her partner to crawl, hop, or otherwise move.

3. Ask partners to switch jobs. This gives the partner who counted a turn to move and the mover a turn to count.

4. Have the teams use a second movement in the same process, with one counting while the other moves, and then switching roles. Ask your students to perform three or more different movements over the same distance, counting the seconds each time.

Ask the teams to examine their results and discuss factors in timing that may have influenced the data. Tell them to determine which actions took the most time and which took the least time. Each child should compare the class's predictions with his or her results, and make a statement about that comparison.

MOVING RIGHT ALONG: Assessment

Examine children's statements about their predictions and their results. Use a checklist for recording less than, greater than, faster, slower, slowest to fastest, and fastest to slowest.

TAKING IT FURTHER: Extensions

✪ Invite students to graph their speeds or graph the number of students who were fastest for each type of movement.

Treasure Measure

STEPPING UP: The Math Behind the Movement

As children estimate distances and lead their blindfolded classmates to treasures around the room, they gain experience using a noncustomary, nonstandard unit of measure—footsteps. In Treasure Measure, students learn to make approximations about footstep length using the length of the blindfolded person's steps as guidance. In addition, they learn how to give directions that follow a sequence as they tell their peers when to step and when to turn.

JUMPING IN: The Activity

Divide the class into small groups. Ask the groups to decide which child will be the treasure Seeker. The other group members serve as Guides. Explain that one of the goals for this activity is for the Guides to help their Seekers locate the treasure following the least number of directions possible. Have one student from each group tally the number of directions given.

When the class is ready, tell them you will be assigning a starting point and a treasure to seek. Ask each group to go to its starting point and blindfold the Seekers. Put a few treasures in different parts of the room and assign each group its treasure. Place them so the treasure Seekers will not have a clear path to the treasure. Have the Guides from each group:

1. Decide which steps their Seeker should take. This decision-making process helps bolster the group's consensus-building skills. Have children take turns giving the directions.

2. Tell their Seeker what to do, such as when to turn or take a step.

3. Wait for the Seeker to move.

4. Record the direction in the tally.

5. Decide what their Seeker should do next, give their Seeker the next direction, record the direction, wait, and continue the process until the Seeker reaches the treasure.

Math Skills and Concepts
nonstandard measurement
estimation
reasoning
communication

Grouping
small groups

Movement
locomotor—walking
perceptual skills

Materials
◆ blindfolds (scarves)
◆ a treasure (pretty boxes or anything fun to find)

If the directions don't accomplish what the group had hoped, then the Guides may provide their Seeker with directions that put him or her back on track. These corrective measures each count as one command. For example, if the instructions take the Seeker too far in one direction and the Guides give the Seeker a direction to turn around and take two steps, in the tally that would count as two directions. (Note: If they said to back up two steps that would save one command.)

After the Seekers have reached their treasures, ask the members of each group to switch roles. Move the treasures so the new Seekers do not know where they are trying to go prior to being blindfolded. Between each search, discuss the experience. Ask: *What have you learned about giving directions that might help everyone improve their scores in the next round of treasure seeking?*

MOVING RIGHT ALONG:
Assessment

Assess how groups came to their decisions as well as what they learned about measuring with footsteps and giving directions. By listening to their work in progress and briefly meeting with groups at the conclusion of the activity, you can quickly gather important insights into these areas.

TAKING IT FURTHER: Extensions

✪ Invite students in each group to draw a treasure map for their seeker. Then have them lead their blindfolded seeker to the treasure. Take this activity one step further by having each group record the route actually taken. The map can be made by using arrows to show when to turn left, turn right, or go back. Dots can record the number of steps predicted and Xs can indicate footsteps actually taken.

Hungry Birds

STEPPING UP: The Math Behind the Movement

In this activity, children sort and then categorize a variety of found objects. Categorizing, a higher-level thinking skill, involves children in recognizing similarities and differences. More than just sorting, categorizing requires that children explain the reasons for their category choices.

JUMPING IN: The Activity

Before you begin, gather a large number of small objects or counters students can use as "food." Plastic bears, pattern blocks, and cubes work well for this activity. Place them on the floor in the center of the room. Mark off the food area with masking tape.

1. Divide the class into four groups. Tell a story of hungry birds (birds feeding in winter, for example) and their discovery of an especially abundant storage of different grains in a park or farmer's field.

2. Explain to your class that each group will be acting as a family of birds. Each family has a home nest in one of the

Math Skills and Concepts
categorizing
problem solving
communication

Grouping
four groups

Movement
locomotor—hopping,
    crawling, etc.
physical fitness—agility

Materials
◆ masking tape
◆ many small objects of
    different colors and shapes

four corners of the classroom (an equal distance from the middle where the pile of counters is located). Tell them that each bird family is a different kind of bird. Some take tiny steps. Others hop, crawl, or make other slow movements. All the birds have beaks. Children can use their pointer finger and thumb as a beak, enabling them to pinch the food tightly as they carry it to the nest.

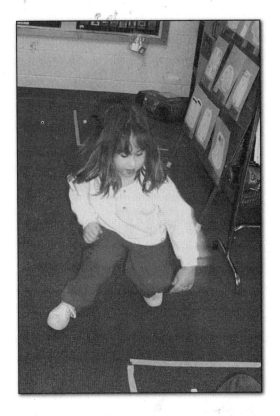

3. Assign one method of body movement to each family of birds. Each time you give a signal, one bird from each group needs to take a turn:

• Leaving the nest to find the food in the marked-off area.

• Using his or her "beak" to carry the objects, one at a time, back to the family nest.

4. Once all the food has been taken from the food area, each family of birds needs to count and sort the food gathered in their nest into categories based on shared attributes. They need to talk about the different "foods" they plan to eat, comparing different attributes: color, shape, and so on.

5. As a class, discuss the activity as a process, deepening students' understanding of the experience. Ask: *How did the bird families work? How and why did you categorize the way you did? What was it like working as a team?*

MOVING RIGHT ALONG: Assessment

Discuss the categories each group identified. Note their ability to create and explain categories based on relevant attributes. Listen carefully to individual children's explanations, observations, and understandings.

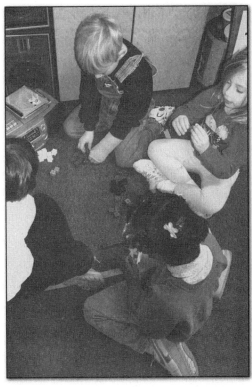

TAKING IT FURTHER: Extensions

✪ Invite your students to explain how their bird family functioned, describe which kind of food they obtained, and tell how much food was collected. Discuss ways in which the body movements of different birds affected food collection. Ask: *Which were the slowest ways to gather food? Fastest? Most interesting?* If some bird families had more class members, talk about the effect that had on collecting food.

 enn Catcher

STEPPING UP: The Math Behind the Movement

Help children "catch on" to the skills of categorizing, sorting, and classifying with Venn Catcher, an activity that has children arrange themselves into sets. From the vantage point of "being the set," children learn to make thoughtful comparisons about sets regarding size, quantity, and common elements.

JUMPING IN: The Activity

Use masking tape to secure two simple yarn shapes, such as a triangle and a square, on the floor large enough for a group of children to stand inside. When you first introduce the activity, make two side-by-side shapes that do not intersect. Explain to the class that they are going to be the sets in each shape. Before you have them move themselves into their set shapes, determine what movements you want the class to use. Simple movements such as hopping, tiptoeing, and jumping work well for this activity. Have students:

1. Discuss ways to categorize the class into two sets, using general descriptors that are neither gender- nor cultural-specific, such as: long/short sleeves, collar/no collar shirt, shoelaces/slip-on shoes, button/pullover shirt, and so on.

2. Have students move to their sets' shapes using the body movements you've specified. For example, if the class is sorting by who is wearing sneakers and who is wearing shoes and all children are supposed to hop, then all sneaker wearers would hop to the square and all of the shoe wearers would hop to the triangle.

Math Skills and Concepts
comparison
classification
problem solving
representation

Grouping
whole class

Movement
locomotor—skipping, hopping, crawling, etc.

Materials
◆ masking tape
◆ yarn

3. Discuss the sets the class has formed. Make comparisons about the number of students in each set: which set has more students, and so on.

4. Have children take turns creating sets and making statements that compare them. Encourage them to help each other decide to which set they belong. After children are in the sets, ask about the number of children not in any set, which set has more children, and whether the sets have anything in common. If some students have trouble deciding where they belong, encourage other children to help them.

5. When students are ready, use shape outlines that overlap. Ask the class to think about what element the two sets might have in common. For example, if the class is to be sorted by hair length and students are supposed to hop to their shape, all the long-haired children would hop to the square and all of the short-haired children would hop to the circle. All of the children with shoulder-length hair would hop to the overlapping area.

MOVING RIGHT ALONG: Assessment

Observe that children are placing themselves in the correct shape. To further evaluate understanding, ask individual children to explain why they need to move to a particular shape.

TAKING IT FURTHER: Extensions

✪ Use tape and yarn to create different shape combinations on the floor. Invite children to decide which set of shapes works best for the elements you name. For example, if you tell them to sort by "students wearing the color red and students wearing the color blue," then students may select two overlapping shapes. That configuration would allow them to place those wearing red in one shape, those wearing blue in the other shape, and those wearing both colors in the overlapping area.

Swirly Streamers

STEPPING UP: The Math Behind the Movement

The whole class will love this whimsical introduction to probability, with children lifting and lowering streamers as they dance to music. By comparing the number of streamers spotted in the up versus the down position when the music stops with the number of dances performed, students gain firsthand experience with an important math concept, probability.

JUMPING IN: The Activity

Explain to students that this activity involves each one of them moving his or her streamer up and down with either hand while dancing creatively to music. When the music stops, that's their signal to hold their bodies still or "freeze" and observe whether their streamers are in the up or down position.

1. Provide each student with one streamer and ask him or her to find a spot in the room where there is plenty of space to dance.

2. As a class, count and record how many children are dancing. Then invite students to predict how many of their streamers will be up and how many will be down when the music stops. Note: Before you begin, establish guidelines about what you mean by "up" versus "down." For instance, identify the shoulders as the marker for determining whether a streamer is up or down. If the streamer is above the shoulder, it is up. If it is below the shoulder, it should be considered down.

3. Encourage students to move the streamer up and down as they interpret the music through dance.

4. Stop the music. Observe students as they "freeze" and quickly determine whether their streamers are above or below their shoulders—up or down.

Math Skills and Concepts
observation of data
predicting outcomes
reasoning
making connections

Grouping
whole class

Movement
using manipulatives
non-locomotor—reaching,
 bending, stretching, etc.

Materials
◆ music
◆ one paper or fabric
 streamer for each child

5. As a class, record the total number of ups and downs. Then discuss the results in relationship to the students' predictions. If the class is ready, this is a good opportunity to invite students to make comparisons using terms such as more than, less than, and how many.

Repeat steps 2–5 several times, recording the class's predictions and results each time. Then add up the numbers to find the totals for predicted and actual ups and downs. Invite your students to share their observations about the two totals. (Observations may include: There was an equal chance that the streamers would be in the up or down position at the close of each dance.)

MOVING RIGHT ALONG: Assessment

While it is important to encourage students to make careful observations, it is also necessary to remind them that a streamer ending up in the up or down position is a chance event. This activity is intended to be an introductory experience, so assessment is best placed on whether students are able to draw meaningful comparisons between what they predicted would happen with the streamers and what actually happened.

TAKING IT FURTHER: Extensions

✪ Double the fun with two streamers instead of one! Provide your students with one streamer for each hand. Record student predictions. Then put on the music, have them dance, and record the results.

✪ Try adding a "middle" streamer position. Be sure to establish guidelines about what you mean by middle. For instance, identify the shoulder as the middle position.

Musical Graph

STEPPING UP: The Math Behind the Movement

An introductory experience with a line graph, this activity builds on young children's experience working with bar graphs and pictographs. Through musical instruments and dance, they gain exposure to the idea of different points along a continuum. Plus, by following the changes recorded in the line graph the class creates, children learn that there are relationships between different visual, kinesthetic, and auditory representational forms. Additionally, Musical Graph is an engaging activity that helps children understand how musical notes form another symbol system.

JUMPING IN: The Activity

Divide the class into small groups: instrumentalists and dancers. Explain to your students that they will be taking turns being instrumentalists and interpretive dancers. Tell them that the class will use the graph as a map of what to do.

Choose three or four instruments with distinct sounds. Give the instruments to the children in the instrumentalists' group. Then assign each instrument a simple shape. For example tambourines could be represented by a circle, triangles by a triangle, and rhythm sticks represented by a rectangle.

Along the horizontal (x-axis) of the graph, draw shapes in the sequence you would like the instrumentalists to play their music. Draw each instrument's assigned shape the same number of times you want students to play beats. For example, two side-by-side circles would mean all of the children playing tambourines should shake their tambourines two times and continue to read the graph until it's their turn to play their instrument again, and so on.

Along the vertical (y-axis) of the graph, draw lines that follow the pattern of music beats and show where, in relative position to the floor and ceiling, the dancers should put their hands as they dance. An ascending line means children should be lifting their hands toward the ceiling. A descending line means children should be lowering their hands toward the floor.

Skills and Concepts
graphing
translating from one
    representation to another
reasoning
communication
representation

Grouping
whole group
two groups

Movement
non-locomotor—stretching,
    swaying, etc.

Materials
◆ rhythm instruments,
    such as rhythm sticks,
    tambourines, and triangles
◆ chart paper
◆ markers

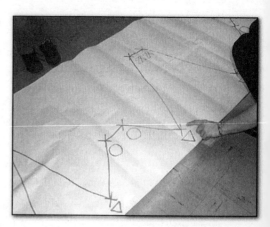

Have every one find a spot where he or she has enough space to move and a good view of the graph. Study the sequence of shapes and hand-position lines as a class to establish what the instrumentalists and dancers are expected to do and when.

When your students are ready:

1. Have the musicians (alone) play the music graph through several times, giving children the experience and the joy of successfully accomplishing something.

2. Have the dancers (alone) rehearse their creative movements as they read the music graph along with you.

3. Put the dancing to music with musicians playing the tune while dancers change their motions in concert with the instruments.

4. Ask students to explain how they know what to do at any point in the music and how they use the music graph to help them.

5. Invite the musicians and dancers to switch roles. Practice with each group separately and then perform again.

After every child in the class has had the role of musician and dancer, discuss the experience. Ask: *What did you find the hardest about following the graph while you were playing or dancing? What did you find easiest?*

MOVING RIGHT ALONG: Assessment

Use a checklist while you observe the children. Note their ability to follow along with the music. From the observations and their comments, determine how well they are working with the idea that if a mark is represented more than once it means to perform the note again.

TAKING IT FURTHER: Extensions

✿ Have students create their own line graphs. Ask them to plan which instruments they'll play, how to show the dance movements on the graph, and how to "conduct" the orchestra using the graph. In this way children can become composers of their own music and involve others in their creative combinations of sound and movement. With experience, students may vary the number of instruments and adjust the graph as needed.

iggle Bars

STEPPING UP: The Math Behind the Movement

In Wiggle Bars children develop their classifying skills by using their personal attributes as data to create a graph. They gather information, sort, and classify as they develop a bar graph.

JUMPING IN: The Activity

Before you begin, choose an open space for this activity. A large, square-shaped carpeted area works well. Place masking tape on the floor as a start line.

Tell your class that they will be constructing a graph to show ways students are alike and different, such as by gender, shirt color, sleeve length, and so on. Tell them the activity is named Wiggle Bars because the children need to move in the bar-graph line. Then have students:

1. Observe each other and discuss similarities and differences in one another's appearance.

2. Form lines in the bar graph, beginning behind the masking-tape start line. (The lines are formed based on the characteristic.)

3. Decide their special way of moving that expresses their special attribute, while maintaining the idea of the bar.

4. Discuss the lengths of the bars.

Take a picture of the Wiggle Bars to have a record of an alternate way of comparing them. Discuss the experience.

MOVING RIGHT ALONG: Assessment

Ask students to draw the Wiggle Bars on paper in order to show the number of people in each bar-graph line. As a class, compare the drawings to the photo. Discuss the differences.

TAKING IT FURTHER: Extensions

✪ Invite children to create a class list of other ways they could perform the Wiggle Bars activity. Ask: *What could we count? Sort?*

✪ Have students work in pairs to sort and graph colored counters, crayons, attribute blocks, and so on.

Math Skills and Concepts
graphing
collecting information
sorting
classifying
reasoning
communication
representation

Grouping
whole class
small groups

Movement
perceptual skills
combined movement
creative movement

Materials
◆ masking tape
◆ camera
◆ recording materials (paper and pencils)